MONEY MATTERS

HOW CONVERSATIONS CAN UNLOCK FINANCIAL FREEDOM

HARRY HEINSEN S.

Acknowledgements

First and foremost, I would like to thank my wife for her unwavering love and support. Thank you honey for always believing in me and encouraging me to follow my dreams, and I couldn't have completed this book without your constant support, encouragement and understanding.

I am also incredibly grateful to my family and friends, who have been there for me every step of the way. Their belief in me and their willingness to listen to my ideas and offer feedback have been invaluable.

I would like to express my gratitude to my editor and publisher, who have worked with me to bring this book to life. Their expertise and guidance have been invaluable, and I am so grateful for their support and encouragement.

I would also like to thank the countless other professionals who have contributed to this book, including proofreaders, designers, and marketers. Your hard work and attention to detail have helped to make this book the best it could be, and I am grateful for your contributions.

Finally, I want to thank my readers. It is an honor to have the opportunity to share my thoughts and ideas with you, and I am deeply grateful for your support and interest in my work.

Disclaimer

This book is meant for informational purposes only and is not intended as investment, legal, or tax advice.

The author is not responsible for any errors or omissions. You should conduct your own research and seek independent advice before making any investment decisions.

This book may include information about past performance of investments, but it is important to note that past performance is not necessarily indicative of future results.

Financial investments carry risks, and it is important you be aware of these risks before making any investment or financial decisions.

If you have any questions about your current financial situation or any investment opportunities please contact a registered financial advisor and do your own independent research before making any decision.

About The Author

Harry Heinsen is an experienced business operator, Fund Manager, and M&A consultant specializing in medium-sized businesses. With an extensive history of working in Latin America, he is skilled in Mergers & Acquisitions, Stock Market Investing, and Management.

Harry currently serves as a Fund Manager for a leading firm in the Dominican Republic and is a partner at Heinsen Global Ventures. Through his firm, **ADVISR**, he focuses on helping entrepreneurs and small business owners avoid the "entrepreneur treadmill"—the cycle of working harder without building transferable value—by generating life-changing value through strategic financial planning.

Contents

1

Breaking The Silence

Money has long been considered one of the final taboos in our society. We often avoid discussing it openly, treating it as a secretive and deeply personal matter. However, this silence surrounding money has significant consequences that can hinder our financial well-being and personal growth. It is time to break that silence and recognize the importance of talking openly about money.

Why We Stay Silent
Our reluctance to have open money discussions comes from a variety of factors, including cultural norms, fear of judgment, and a lack of financial education. Many of us were taught as children that discussing money is impolite or even shameful. As a result, we carry this mindset into adulthood, avoiding conversations about our salaries, our debts, or our financial struggles. But this silence only perpetuates the cycle of financial ignorance and interferes with our ability to make informed decisions. For the entrepreneur, this silence is the engine of the "entrepreneur treadmill." We wear a "success

mask," fearing that if we speak about our financial challenges, we will be exposed as failures. This mask keeps us running in place, working harder to cover up the cracks rather than fixing the foundation.

The Detrimental Effect of Avoiding the "Talk"
Avoiding money conversations has a tangible, negative impact on our lives:

> *Relational Breakdown:* Money plays a significant role in romantic partnerships, friendships, and family dynamics. Without open communication, money leads to misunderstandings, resentment, and the breakdown of these relationships.
> *Creation of Tension:* Without honest communication about financial goals, expectations, and responsibilities, we risk creating unnecessary conflict.
> *Stagnant Personal Growth:* When we don't discuss money, we miss out on opportunities to learn from others and gain new perspectives.
> *Ignorance of Strategy:* We stay unaware of helpful strategies for budgeting, investing, or debt management that could significantly impact our lives.

The Power of Vulnerability

It is natural to feel vulnerable when discussing our financial situations, as it exposes our successes and, more importantly, our failures and challenges. However, embracing this vulnerability and engaging in open conversations can be empowering. It allows us to share our experiences, seek advice, and learn from those who have navigated similar financial situations before us.

Open communication builds trust and understanding. When we openly discuss our financial goals, fears, and challenges with our partners or business associates, we create an environment of mutual support. We can work together toward common financial objectives and provide guidance when it is needed most.

Shifting the Perception

Society needs to shift its perception and recognize that talking about money should not only be acceptable but is necessary for our financial well-being. This change starts with us as individuals sharing our experiences and encouraging others to do the same.

By discussing money openly, we bridge the gap in financial knowledge and empower ourselves with practical insights and strategies. We can share resources, recommend courses, and encourage ongoing learning. It is time to break the silence, step off the treadmill, and start talking about money.

Transparency Toolkit: The "Icebreaker"
Breaking the silence is the hardest part. Use these scripts to start the conversation today:

> To a Spouse/Partner: > *"I've realized recently that I've been holding onto our financial stress alone because I didn't want to worry you. I think we're both feeling the pressure of the 'treadmill' lately, and I want to change that. Can we set a time this week to just look at where we are—honestly and without judgment?"*
> To a Business Partner: > *"I want to make sure we aren't just 'staying busy' but actually building long-term value. I'd like us to have a transparent audit of our cash flow and personal goals. If we're going to grow, we need to be on the same page about the numbers."*
> To a Close Friend or Mentor: > *"I've been feeling like I'm running in circles with my finances lately. I'm curious—how do you handle balancing your personal financial goals with the demands of your business? I'd value your perspective on how you stay grounded."*

2

The Power Of Transparency

Transparency is a powerful force that can transform our relationships and enhance our financial well-being. When we choose to be open about our financial situations, goals, and challenges, we build trust, understanding, and a solid foundation for collaboration. For the business owner, this transparency is the first step in moving from a state of constant "running" to a state of actual value generation. By opening up the books—both personal and professional—you create the clarity needed to step off the entrepreneur treadmill.

Overcoming the Fear of Judgment
One of the main reasons we shy away from transparency is the fear of judgment. We worry about what others might think of our income, our debts, or our spending habits. This fear often stems from a deep-rooted societal belief that our financial worth defines our value as individuals. However, this mindset is flawed and limiting. To embrace transparency, we must recognize that our financial situation does not define our worth as human beings; we are more than just numbers on a balance sheet. By separating our self-worth from our financial status, we open ourselves up

to honest conversations and genuine connections.

Inviting Others into Your Journey
When you choose to be transparent, you invite others into your financial journey. This openness creates an environment of trust and allows you to share your successes, failures, and challenges with the people who matter most.

> *Fostering Empathy:* Sharing the reality of the "treadmill" fosters support and collaboration.
> *Aligning Goals:* When everyone has a clear understanding of each other's aspirations, it becomes easier to work together toward common objectives.
> *Joint Decision-Making:* Transparency enables decisions that prioritize collective well-being and long-term financial stability.

Tapping into Collective Wisdom
Transparency allows us to identify areas where we can provide or receive support. When we are comfortable discussing our challenges, we can tap into the collective wisdom of our connections. We can learn from those who have overcome similar obstacles or seek advice from those with more expertise. This collaborative approach

strengthens our financial knowledge and empowers us to make better-informed decisions.

Transparency in Responsibilities and Conflict
Transparency also extends to our financial responsibilities within our relationships. Whether sharing household expenses or setting long-term goals, open communication is key. When all parties understand their roles and obligations, it promotes fairness, trust, and shared accountability.
Proactively discussing financial expectations, boundaries, and concerns allows us to address potential conflicts before they escalate. By fostering a safe and non-judgmental space, we can encourage open sharing where everyone feels comfortable talking about their financial journeys.

Transparency in the Workplace
Clear money conversations at work are equally important. Discussions about promotions, bonuses, and career development are essential for a healthy workplace culture. When employees understand the factors influencing these decisions, they can better advocate for themselves and navigate their career paths. Open communication helps create a culture of transparency, trust, and empowerment.

Taking the First Steps

To embrace transparency, you must acknowledge the feelings of discomfort and remind yourself that transparency is a strength, not a weakness.

> *Reflect:* Consider if your discomfort is rooted in societal expectations or a fear of vulnerability.
> *Practice Small Steps:* Initiate money conversations with people you trust.
> *Share Goals and Seek Advice:* Discuss a specific financial challenge or goal to experience the positive impact of opening up.
> *Exercise Discretion:* Being transparent does not mean oversharing or disclosing sensitive information to everyone. Share only what feels appropriate and comfortable for you.

Transparency is about being open and honest, not about divulging every detail of your life. By harnessing the power of transparency, you can align your goals, seek support, and unlock the full potential of your financial journey.

3

Money And Relationships

Money is intricately woven into the fabric of our relationships, influencing romantic partnerships, friendships, and family dynamics in profound ways—even when we don't see it. The way we handle and communicate about money can either strengthen or strain our connections. For many, money is a leading cause of conflict and stress, stemming from differences in spending habits, goals, and attitudes.

In the context of the entrepreneur treadmill, this silence at home is often what keeps the motor running. When an entrepreneur is trapped in the cycle of "more work," they often leave their partner in the dark about the true financial health of the business or the actual cost of their time. Breaking this silence is the only way to build a healthy, sustainable future.

Prioritizing Open Communication
To build healthy financial dynamics, we must prioritize open and non-judgmental communication. This starts by creating a safe space where both partners can discuss their aspirations, concerns, and values without fear of criticism. This requires active listening and setting aside judgment of one another's perspectives.

Navigating Disparities and Imbalances
A common challenge in relationships is managing disparities in income or resources, which can lead to imbalances in decision-making and power dynamics.

> *Empathy is Key:* Recognize that each person brings unique financial circumstances and challenges.
>
> *Foster Equality:* If one partner earns significantly more, it is crucial to maintain an environment of mutual respect.
>
> *Proportional Management:* Discussing how to divide expenses—perhaps proportionally or through a joint budget—can help alleviate feelings of unfairness or resentment.

Aligning Goals and Managing Debt
Financial goals play a pivotal role in shaping a relationship. It is essential for partners to discuss individual goals and find common ground to work toward shared objectives, such as saving for a home, retirement, or supporting causes.

> *Debt as a Partnership:* Many individuals carry personal debts like student loans or mortgages. Discussing these obligations openly and creating a plan to tackle them individually or together provides relief and a sense of partnership.

Shared Responsibility: Approaching debt as a shared burden ensures both partners are actively engaged in the solution. Even if finances are managed separately, understanding your partner's situation reduces the risk of misinterpreting their financial decisions later.

Preparing for the Unexpected
Financial challenges like job loss or medical emergencies can arise unexpectedly. These situations strain relationships if they aren't approached with supportive communication. Developing contingency plans, building emergency funds, and discussing potential hardships beforehand helps partners navigate these crises together.

Money in Friendships and Family
Beyond romantic partners, money influences friendships and family.

Friendships: Maintain healthy friendships by approaching money with sensitivity and avoiding assumptions based on income levels. Friends can also empower one another by sharing financial strategies and resources.
Parenting: Parents play a crucial role in shaping their children's financial attitudes.

Discussing money early helps instill responsibility and healthy habits.

Aging Parents: Conversations with aging parents regarding retirement or long-term care should be approached with respect and empathy for their autonomy.

Legacy Planning: In families with wealth, open conversations about wills and trusts can prevent future conflicts and ensure a smooth transition of assets.

Strategies for Effective Financial Conversations

To foster healthy dynamics, consider implementing these strategies:

Regular Check-ins: Schedule dedicated times to discuss finances and review progress toward goals.

Share Responsibilities: Distribute tasks like bill payment or investment research based on each partner's strengths.

Create a Joint Budget: Design a budget together that reflects your shared priorities.

Practice Transparency: Be open about your income, debts, and assets to build trust and allow for informed joint decisions.

Seek Professional Help: If disagreements become overwhelming, consider a financial advisor or couples therapist to navigate complex dynamics.

Communication is the foundation of healthy financial dynamics. By embracing transparency and mutual support, your relationships can thrive even while you work toward your financial goals.

4

Financial Education

empowering minds and wallets

Financial education is a powerful tool that empowers individuals to make informed decisions, take control of their finances, and build a secure future. Yet, it remains a significant gap in traditional education systems and is often overlooked in personal development. For many, this gap is the invisible tether that keeps them on the entrepreneur treadmill. Without a solid understanding of how wealth is built and protected, an entrepreneur can spend a lifetime generating revenue without ever achieving true financial independence.

Beyond Basic Management

Financial education goes far beyond simply understanding basic concepts of money management. It encompasses a wide range of strategic topics, including:

> *Budgeting and Saving:* Developing effective skills to ensure income is allocated wisely.
> *Strategic Investing:* Learning to build wealth over time to secure a financial future outside of your primary business.
> *Debt Management:* Avoiding the pitfalls of excessive borrowing and developing efficient repayment strategies.
> *Retirement and Insurance:* Planning for the long term and protecting assets against the unexpected.

The Power of Informed Decision-Making

The fundamental benefit of financial education is the ability to make informed financial decisions. When you have a solid understanding of financial principles, you can evaluate your options, weigh risks against rewards, and make choices that align with your long-term goals. This literacy empowers you to navigate a variety of financial situations and adapt when the economic landscape shifts.

In an ever-changing environment, resilience and adaptability are crucial. With knowledge of market trends and investment options, you can make the necessary adjustments to your financial plans to take advantage of new opportunities.

Taking Responsibility for Your Literacy
While governments and educational institutions should play a role in promoting financial literacy, the ultimate responsibility for financial education falls on you. Fortunately, we live in an age where resources for self-learning are abundant:

> *Self-Directed Learning:* Books, online courses, podcasts, and workshops provide accessible, comprehensive information.
> *Interactive Tools:* Online platforms offer calculators to help you understand complex concepts like compound interest and retirement planning.
> *Professional Seminars:* Many financial institutions and employers now offer workshops and wellness programs to enhance the literacy of their customers and collaborators.

The Generational Off-Ramp
Parents have a significant influence on the financial education of future generations. By incorporating money conversations into daily life, you can instill healthy financial habits in your children early on. Teaching them about budgeting, saving, and the difference between needs and

wants sets a strong foundation for their financial future—ensuring they don't grow up to find themselves on a treadmill of their own.

Turning Knowledge into Action
Financial education is an ongoing process because the financial landscape is constantly evolving. However, to maximize the benefits of this education, you must combine knowledge with action. Learning about financial concepts is only valuable if you apply that knowledge to your own situation. Setting goals, creating budgets, and implementing investment strategies are the essential steps in putting your education into practice.

Financial education is not a luxury; it is a necessity in today's complex financial landscape. It is the key to building a secure future and contributing to a stable economy.

Transparency Toolkit: The "Strategic Learner"
Education is a collaborative process. Use these scripts to start a conversation about expanding your financial knowledge:

> To a Financial Advisor:
> *"I understand how to run my business, but I want to be more literate in how to build wealth outside of it. Can we spend our next session focusing on 'Wealth IQ' specifically how to diversify my assets*

so I'm not 100% dependent on my company's daily performance?"

To a Business Partner:

"I've been doing some reading on business value generation, and I've realized there's a gap in my financial education regarding our long-term exit strategy. I'd like to take a course or bring in a consultant to help us both understand the numbers that make our business an actual transferable asset."

To your Children:

"I want to start a new tradition. Once a month, let's look at a different 'Money Matter' together. Today, let's look at how compound interest works it's basically a way to make your money work for you so you don't have to work as hard later."

5

Overcoming Financial Challenges

Financial challenges are an inevitable part of the entrepreneurial journey. Whether it is unexpected business expenses, a sudden reduction in personal income, or the weight of mounting debt, navigating these situations can feel overwhelming. However, with the right mindset and a commitment to open communication, it is possible to overcome these hurdles and emerge stronger on the other side. For the entrepreneur, a financial challenge isn't just a hurdle; it is a test of the systems designed to keep you off the treadmill.

Income Volatility and the Owner's Draw
One of the most significant challenges an entrepreneur faces is the fluctuation of personal income. Unlike a traditional employee, your "paycheck" is often tied to the immediate health of the business. When income reduces due to economic downturns or internal changes, immediate action is required to stabilize your personal financial situation.

> *Assess and Realign:* Start by assessing your available resources and creating a budget that reflects your current income level.
> *Prioritize Essentials:* Focus on housing, utilities, and food while identifying non-essential areas to cut back.
> *Alternative Streams:* Explore freelance work or part-time opportunities to bridge the gap during lean periods.
> *Utilize Support:* Do not shy away from government assistance programs or unemployment benefits that can provide temporary relief.

Debt Management as an Off-Ramp

Debt can be a significant burden that hinders your progress toward financial freedom. Managing it effectively requires a clear picture of your obligations, including balances and interest rates.

Repayment Strategies: Use the snowball method (paying off smallest debts first) or the avalanche method (prioritizing high-interest debt) to gain momentum.

Communication is Key: If you are struggling, talk to your creditors. Many are willing to create alternative payment plans or offer temporary relief if you are proactive.

Consolidation: Explore refinancing or consolidation to lower interest rates and simplify your monthly obligations.

Building Resilience (The Liquidity Trap)

Building an emergency fund is your primary defense against the unexpected. It serves as a safety net for medical bills, car repairs, or home maintenance that could otherwise derail your business focus.

Realistic Goals: Set a savings target and contribute consistently, even in small amounts.

Automate Growth: Set up automatic transfers to your savings account to ensure consistency.

Redirect Funds: Cut back on non-essential spending and redirect that capital into your resilience fund.

Strategic Goal Setting

Success requires clear financial goals and a solid plan. For the entrepreneur, this means distinguishing between short-term survival and long-term exit strategy.

> *Short-term:* Build an emergency fund and pay off high-interest debt.
> *Medium-term:* Save for a down payment or business expansion.
> *Long-term:* Focus on retirement, investments, and legacy planning.
> *Seek Guidance:* A financial advisor can help break these goals into actionable milestones.

Mindset and Well-Being

Overcoming challenges requires a resilient mindset. It is essential to view obstacles as opportunities for growth rather than personal failures.

> *Abundance Mindset:* Focus on possibilities and what you have, rather than dwelling on lack.
> *Self-Care:* Prioritize your physical and mental health during stressful times.

Holistic Well-Being: Remember that financial success is meaningless if your emotional and psychological health suffers in the process.

Transparency Toolkit: The "Crisis Communication"
When the storm hits, the worst thing you can do is go silent. Use these scripts to navigate the pressure:

To a Spouse (Income Reduction):
"I've been looking at the numbers for this month, and we're going to see a reduction in the owner's draw because of a temporary dip in the business. I want to sit down and look at our 'essentials' list so we can adjust our personal budget together until things stabilize."

To a Creditor (Debt Pressure):
"I am currently facing some cash flow challenges and want to be proactive about my obligations. Can we discuss a temporary alternative payment plan or a hardship deferment while I restructure my repayment strategy?"

To a Business Partner (Strategic Planning):
"We're hitting some financial friction, and I think it's time we re-evaluate our medium-term goals. Let's sit down with an advisor to make sure our current debt levels aren't putting our long-term exit strategy at risk."

6

Parenting And Money

Teaching children about money is one of the most critical aspects of their education, yet it is often the most overlooked. By introducing financial concepts early, we provide them with the tools to make informed decisions and avoid the traps of financial ignorance. For the entrepreneur, this isn't just about teaching "savings"; it is about ensuring our children don't inherit the "entrepreneur treadmill" mindset—where they equate worth solely with hard work rather than strategic value.

The Pillars of Financial Parenting
When we talk to our children about money, we are building four essential foundations:

> *Financial Literacy:* This is the bedrock of sound decision-making, covering budgeting, saving, and understanding the value of a dollar.
> *Responsibility and Accountability:* Children must learn that money is earned and should be spent wisely, understanding the consequences of their financial choices.
> *Healthy Habits:* Early exposure helps children avoid the pitfalls of "bad debt" and impulsive purchasing.

Independence: Knowledge fosters the confidence to manage their own money and set personal goals as they grow.

Practical Strategies for Every Age
The goal is to keep an open, age-appropriate discussion about financial responsibilities.

1. The Power of Tangible Money (Ages 5–10)
Start early with simple discussions about coin values. When children are ready, involve them in everyday activities like grocery shopping.

> *The Budget Exercise:* Give your child a small budget to buy their snacks for the week. Allow them the liberty to make choices within that limit.
> *Use Cash, Not Cards:* Children cannot grasp the concept of a credit card; they only see a card being tapped to receive a reward. They need to see the money dwindle and eventually run out to understand that resources are finite.

2. The Strategic Teenager (Ages 11–17)
As children grow, allow them to see the "business" of the household.

> *Collaborative Planning:* Involve them in budgeting for special occasions, like a

family trip. While they don't make the final call, it helps them understand the scope of what is possible.

Shared Responsibilities: Make them responsible for specific monthly bills, such as a streaming service or their telephone bill.

Total Transparency: By their senior year of high school, a child should understand the cost of running the household. They will soon be running their own lives; it is better they learn the "hard way" while still under your roof.

3. Allowances and Entrepreneurial Spirit

Provide allowances through opportunities to earn. This isn't about labor; it's about teaching the relationship between work and money.

The Accomplishment High: Summer jobs, like lifeguarding or camp monitoring, boost self-esteem and independence. There is power in knowing you earned the money for your own movie ticket or lunch.

Encouraging Independence: Foster an entrepreneurial spirit by encouraging them to mow lawns, wash cars, or sell handmade crafts.

Learning from Failure: Set the boundaries, then get out of the way. Let them make bad financial decisions and discuss what they could have done differently.

4. Leading by Example

Children learn by observing your behavior. If you practice responsible habits—budgeting, saving, and avoiding impulsive buys—they will follow suit.

As parents, we often want to hide our daily struggles and sacrifices to protect our children's "bliss". However, children can tell when parents are stressed, and without a conversation, they may fear it is their fault. Involving them with age-appropriate information is the best way to prepare them for tomorrow. Raising financially literate children is an investment in their future, empowering them to take control of their well-being and build a prosperous life.

7

Money And Mental Health

Money plays a significant role in our lives, impacting various aspects of our well-being, including our mental health. While we often view finances as a series of spreadsheets and bank balances, the reality is that our emotional state is deeply tied to our financial security. Financial stress can take a heavy toll on our mental well-being, leading to anxiety, depression, and other emotional struggles.

For the entrepreneur, this connection is even more intense. The "entrepreneur treadmill"—the relentless cycle of working harder without building true value—is a primary driver of founder burnout. When we are stuck in this cycle, we don't just feel tired; we feel trapped. The silence surrounding our financial reality acts as a pressure cooker, exacerbating the stress until it impacts every facet of our lives.

The Emotional Toll of Financial Stress
Financial difficulties often trigger a range of powerful emotions, including fear, frustration, and shame. When we are faced with constant worry about money or mounting debts, the uncertainty about the future leads to persistent levels of anxiety and a negative impact on our overall mood.

This stress doesn't stay confined to the office. It manifests physically and psychologically:

> *Physical Disruption:* Financial stress is often felt through the disruption of sleep patterns, leaving us exhausted and less capable of handling the demands of the day.

Emotional Regulation: It impairs our ability to regulate our emotions, making us more reactive and less resilient in the face of normal business challenges.

Relational Strain: Our relationships suffer as financial difficulties lead to conflicts and communication breakdowns with partners, family members, and friends.

The Shame of the Treadmill

One of the most damaging aspects of financial stress is the sense of shame and inadequacy it creates. Entrepreneurs, in particular, often compare themselves to their peers and perceive their financial struggles as personal failures. This leads to a sharp decline in self-esteem and a negative self-image.

We believe that if the business isn't providing the freedom we promised ourselves, then we have failed as leaders. This is the shame of the treadmill. We hide the struggle to maintain a facade of success, but that very secrecy prevents us from finding the solutions that could set us free.

Seeking Support: The Path to Healing

During times of financial stress, it is essential to prioritize your mental health and utilize available resources to address both the practical and emotional aspects of the challenge.

Leveraging Your Inner Circle

Reaching out to loved ones is a crucial first step. Sharing your worries and anxieties with trusted family members and friends can have a profound impact on your well-being. Opening up allows those closest to you to provide emotional support and understanding, reminding you that you are not alone in your journey. Often, loved ones bring a fresh perspective and can help you brainstorm practical solutions, such as budgeting tips or cost-cutting strategies.

Professional Financial Guidance
Consulting with financial professionals, such as planners or counselors, offers expertise tailored to your specific situation. These professionals can:

> *Create a Plan:* Help you develop a comprehensive budget that aligns with your income and long-term aspirations.
> *Objective Analysis:* Provide an objective view of your situation, identifying areas where you may be overspending or missing opportunities to increase savings.
> *Literacy and Confidence:* Explain complex financial concepts in a simplified manner, empowering you to navigate the financial landscape with confidence.

Mental Health Support

If financial stress begins to overwhelm you, it is vital to seek support from mental health professionals. Therapists and counselors provide a safe, non-judgmental space to express your fears.

> *Coping Strategies:* They can teach you stress management techniques, relaxation exercises, and mindfulness practices.
> *Reframing Mindsets:* A professional can help you explore the underlying emotional issues contributing to your relationship with money, helping you reframe negative thought patterns and build resilience.

By reaching out to loved ones, seeking professional guidance, and engaging in open conversations, you gain the knowledge and strategies needed to navigate financial stress. Together, we can break the silence surrounding money-related anxieties and foster a culture of understanding and empowerment. Remember, prioritizing your mental well-being is not a distraction from your financial goals; it is the foundation upon which true, sustainable wealth is built.

8

Talking Entrepreneurship

Entrepreneurship is often romanticized as the ultimate path to freedom, yet for many, it becomes a high-speed treadmill. You work longer hours, chase more leads, and manage more people, yet your personal financial security remains stagnant. The business grows, but you are more tied to it than ever.

At **ADVISR** , I see this daily: brilliant operators who are "running" but not "moving". The off-ramp from this treadmill isn't more work—it is more conversation. In this chapter, we will explore how talking openly about finances allows entrepreneurs to manage risks, align with partners, and build a business that generates actual value rather than just more work.

The Silence that Powers the Treadmill
The "Entrepreneur Treadmill" is fueled by silence. We often avoid discussing our business finances because we fear judgment or feel our financial worth defines our value as individuals. This leads to several critical errors:

> *The Budgeting Blind Spot:* Without open discussion, we cannot effectively plan resources or manage cash flow.

Lack of Accountability: Talking about financial goals and milestones allows us to track progress and hold ourselves accountable for meeting objectives.

The "Performance" Mask: When we don't talk about our challenges, we miss out on the collective wisdom of our network that could help us overcome obstacles.

Strategic Conversations with Partners and Investors

If you are in a partnership, money is the most common cause of friction. Clear communication is vital for aligning expectations and financial contributions.

Investor Communication: If you are seeking growth, you must present a compelling case. This requires a transparent understanding of your financial dynamics and growth potential.

Partnership Alignment: Open dialogue ensures all partners are on the same page, reducing the risk of misunderstandings that lead to business breakdowns.

Refining the Strategy: By discussing revenue streams, cost structures, and pricing models, you can move from "surviving" to "thriving".

Managing Risks: Your Financial Safety Net

The treadmill feels dangerous because there is no safety net. Managing financial risks through transparency is how you build that net:

Build a Financial Cushion: Access to emergency funds or backup financing is essential to navigate unexpected economic downturns or expenses.

Diversify Revenue: Relying on a single source of income is risky. Explore new markets or customer segments to spread that risk.

Continuous Monitoring: Regularly review financial performance and adjust expenses. If you aren't talking about the numbers, you won't see the treadmill coming until you're exhausted.

Building a Network for Financial Guidance

You do not have to run this race alone. A supportive network is the ultimate "treadmill" off-ramp.

Mentors and Advisors: Identify experienced guides who can provide strategic advice on financial management and tax planning.

Peer Support Groups: Mastermind groups of fellow entrepreneurs provide a safe space to discuss the financial challenges no one else understands.

Professional Collaboration: Work with accountants and financial planners to ensure your business strategy aligns with your personal long-term financial security.

Money Matters Note: Breaking the silence about your business's financial reality is an act of bravery, not failure. By the end of this journey, you will be equipped with the confidence to take control of your financial destiny and achieve true freedom from the treadmill.

Remember, entrepreneurship is a journey of continuous learning. Embrace the conversation, seek guidance, and stop running in place.

9

Navigating The World Of Credit And Debt

Credit and debt play significant roles in our financial lives. When used wisely, they are powerful tools that allow us to make major purchases, invest in our education, or start businesses. However, mismanaging credit and falling into excessive debt can have detrimental consequences on our financial well-being. For the entrepreneur, the distinction is even sharper: debt is either the fuel for the off-ramp (growth) or the weight that keeps you stuck on the treadmill (survival).

Understanding Credit as Your Financial Reputation
Credit is an agreement between a borrower and a lender, granting access to funds with the expectation of repayment over time. Understanding how it works is essential, as it impacts your ability to secure loans, obtain favorable interest rates, and can even affect your employment and housing opportunities.

> *Credit Reports and Scores:* Agencies compile your credit history into reports used by lenders to assess your creditworthiness. These reports include your payment history, outstanding debts, and public records like bankruptcies. Lenders use this to calculate your credit score, typically ranging from 300 to 850.
> *Building and Maintaining Good Credit:* This is a long-term process requiring responsible behavior. You can build history by opening a credit card or obtaining a small loan, making timely payments, and keeping credit utilization low.
> *Monitoring Your Credit:* Regularly review your reports to ensure accuracy and

identify potential issues. You are entitled
to a free annual credit report from major
agencies.

Managing Debt Effectively
Managing debt is crucial for maintaining stability
and minimizing stress. Whether it is student loans,
credit card balances, or business-related
mortgages, you need a clear strategy to ensure debt
doesn't become a "lash" that forces you to run
faster on the treadmill.

>*The Repayment Plan:* Assess your
>outstanding debts, including balances,
>interest rates, and minimum payments.
>Develop a plan that suits your goals, such
>as the snowball method (smallest debts
>first) or the avalanche method (highest
>interest rates first).
>*Budgeting and Cash Flow:* Create a realistic
>budget to allocate funds for debt while
>covering essential expenses. Redirect
>funds from non-essential spending toward
>repayment and monitor your cash flow
>closely.
>*Negotiating with Creditors:* If you face
>difficulty, contact your creditors
>immediately. Many are willing to discuss
>alternative payment plans or temporary
>relief options for those facing hardship.

Consolidation and Refinancing: Consider combining multiple debts into a single loan or replacing existing loans with new ones offering better terms. This can simplify repayment and reduce overall interest costs.

Making Informed Borrowing Decisions

Borrowing money is a significant decision that requires caution and careful consideration. It should never be a reflex to solve a temporary cash flow problem; it must be a strategic choice.

Assess Your Situation: Determine if taking on additional debt is truly necessary or feasible based on your income and long-term goals.

Understand Your Options: Familiarize yourself with different types of credit—personal loans, credit cards, or lines of credit—and evaluate their unique features and terms.

Compare Interest Rates: Even a small difference in rates can significantly impact the total cost of borrowing. Consider the total repayment amount and any additional fees.

Read the Fine Print: Carefully read and understand all loan agreements, focusing on repayment schedules and penalties, before signing.

Borrow Responsibly: Only borrow what you need and can comfortably repay, avoiding debt for unnecessary luxuries.

Avoiding Predatory Lending Practices
Be vigilant against predatory practices that exploit vulnerable borrowers through excessively high rates, hidden fees, or aggressive collection tactics.

Research Lenders: Verify their credentials and reputation before engaging. Ensure they are licensed and regulated.
Seek Legal Advice: If you suspect unfair practices, seek advice to understand your rights under consumer protection laws.
Report Abuse: Report predatory lenders to regulatory authorities to protect others from similar practices.

Transparency Toolkit: The "Credit & Leverage"
Debt thrives in the dark. Use these scripts to bring transparency to your borrowing:

To a Lender (Rate Negotiation):
"I have been reviewing my credit report and my history of timely payments with you. Based on current market rates and my improved credit score, I'd like to discuss lowering the interest rate on my current line of credit to ensure it remains a sustainable growth tool for my business."

To a Business Partner (Strategic Debt Audit):

"I want to review our current business debt. Is this debt helping us build an asset that can eventually run without us, or is it just paying for our 'spot' on the treadmill? Let's look at the ROI of our current loans and see if we need to refinance to prioritize our exit strategy."

To a Spouse (Credit Goals):

"I want us to have the best possible credit score so we can access lower rates for our future plans. Can we sit down this weekend and look at our credit reports together? I want to make sure we're both aware of where we stand and how we can improve our 'financial reputation' as a team."

10

Planning For The Future

retirement and long term financial security Planning for retirement and long-term financial security is essential to ensure a comfortable and fulfilling future. It involves setting clear financial goals, creating a retirement plan, and making informed decisions to build a nest egg that sustains you throughout your post-work years. For the entrepreneur, however, retirement planning has a unique dimension: your business is often your largest asset, but it only contributes to your "nest egg" if you have a plan to step off the treadmill and turn it into a transferable asset.

The Critical Need for a Plan

Retirement planning is the roadmap for accumulating the necessary funds to support your lifestyle once you stop working. It allows you to maintain your desired standard of living and financial independence during your golden years. Several factors make this planning urgent:

> *Increasing Life Expectancy:* People are living longer, meaning retirement can last for decades. You must ensure you have sufficient funds to cover prolonged healthcare and lifestyle costs.
>
> *A Shifting Pension Landscape:* Traditional employer-provided pensions are becoming rare, placing the responsibility of saving and investing squarely on the individual.
>
> *Inflation:* Over time, inflation erodes the purchasing power of money. Your plan must account for rising costs to ensure your savings keep up with future needs.

Assessing Your Needs and Setting Goals

A successful plan begins by defining what your retirement looks like and what it will cost:

Lifestyle and Expenses: Estimate costs for housing, healthcare, leisure, and travel. This assessment helps gauge the total savings required to support your vision.
Retirement Age: Deciding when to retire affects how long you have to save and how long your savings must last.
Healthcare and Benefits: Understand potential Social Security benefits and research healthcare options like Medicare or supplemental insurance. Factor these into your income and expense projections.

Building the Nest Egg: Saving and Investing
The earlier you start, the more you can leverage compounding returns.

Retirement Accounts: Utilize employer-sponsored plans (like 401(k)s) or Individual Retirement Accounts (IRAs). These offer tax advantages that significantly boost long-term savings.
Diversification: Build a portfolio that balances risk and return across stocks, bonds, and mutual funds. This is especially vital for entrepreneurs who must avoid having their entire net worth tied up in their business.

Regular Adjustments: Review your portfolio periodically to ensure it still aligns with your goals and risk tolerance.

Long-Term Care and Estate Planning

A secure future also means planning for the possibility of chronic illness or disability.

Long-Term Care Options: Research the costs of in-home care, assisted living, or nursing homes. Long-term care insurance can provide a vital financial safety net for you and your family.

Estate Planning: This includes creating a will, establishing power of attorney, and potentially setting up trusts to protect assets and ensure your wishes are carried out.

Breaking the Taboo: The Legacy Conversation

Breaking the silence surrounding retirement and estate planning is a requirement for future security. Creating a safe, supportive environment where family members can share their thoughts and feelings helps reduce the stigma associated with these sensitive subjects.

Openly communicating your long-term care plans and desires with your loved ones ensures everyone is on the same page and can assist in making informed decisions when the time comes. By creating an open and accepting family culture, you ensure that future generations feel comfortable discussing these matters without fear of judgment.

Transparency Toolkit: The "Legacy & Exit"
Planning for the end of your career is the ultimate way to step off the treadmill. Use these scripts to start the conversation:

> To a Spouse (Lifestyle and Care): > *"I want to make sure that as we get older, we are both taken care of without putting a burden on our kids. Can we sit down this weekend to look at our long-term care options and discuss what our 'ideal' retirement lifestyle actually costs?"*
> To a Business Partner (Exit Planning): > *"We've built something great, but I want to make sure the business is an asset that can eventually run without us. Let's talk to a specialist about an exit strategy—not because I want to leave today, but because I want the freedom to choose when I do."*
> To Adult Children (The Inheritance Talk): > *"I want to be transparent with you about our estate plan. We've set up a will and a trust to make sure things are handled smoothly later on. I'd like to share the basics with you so there are no surprises and you understand our intentions for the family legacy."*

11

Building Wealth Through Investments

stock, bonds and real estate
Building wealth through investments is the fundamental strategy for achieving long-term financial success and, more importantly, securing your exit from the entrepreneur treadmill. While your business may be your primary passion, true financial freedom comes from having assets that work for you independently of your daily labor. To achieve this, you must engage in open conversations about three key asset classes: stocks, bonds, and real estate.

1. Stocks: Moving from Operator to Owner
Investing in stocks allows you to participate in the growth and success of established businesses without being the one running them. However, successful stock investing requires a shift from an "entrepreneurial" mindset to an "investor" mindset.

> *The Risk/Return Conversation:* Stocks offer significant return potential but come with market volatility. Talking to a professional helps you conduct fundamental analysis—assessing a company's financial health and growth prospects—to manage this risk.

Strategic Diversification: You shouldn't just "buy what you know." Diversifying across different industries and geographies reduces the impact of any single company's performance on your wealth.
Passive vs. Active: Decide whether you want to match market performance through index funds (passive) or attempt to outperform it through individual stock selection (active).
The Long-Term Perspective: Stock investing is a marathon. Open communication with an advisor helps you stay focused on long-term goals and avoid impulsive decisions during short-term market movements.

2. Bonds: Creating Predictable Stability
Bonds are debt securities where you lend money to governments or corporations in exchange for regular interest payments. In a wealth-building strategy, they provide the "ballast" for your portfolio.

Understanding the Terms: Conversations about bonds should focus on maturity dates, coupon rates, and credit ratings. Maturity is the time until you get your principal back, while the coupon rate is your interest.

Risk Management: Credit ratings from agencies like Moody's or Standard & Poor's help you assess the risk of a bond issuer defaulting.

Diversification: Just as with stocks, you should spread your bond investments across different issuers and maturities to manage interest rate risk. Bond funds can offer a convenient way to access a diversified portfolio.

3. *Real Estate:* Building Tangible Wealth

Real estate provides a combination of cash flow and long-term appreciation. It is often the most comfortable "off-ramp" for entrepreneurs because it is a tangible asset.

Investment Options: You can choose direct ownership through rental properties, or use indirect methods like Real Estate Investment Trusts (REITs) and crowdfunding platforms.

Defining the Strategy: Are you looking for steady income (buy-and-hold) or quick capital gains (fix-and-flip)?. Each strategy has a different risk profile and requires a different level of time commitment.

Market Analysis: Thorough research into local regulations, economic indicators, and supply/demand dynamics is essential before committing capital.

4. Balancing Your "Exit" Portfolio

Building wealth isn't about picking one winner; it's about creating a balanced portfolio that aligns with your specific risk tolerance and your goal of leaving the treadmill.

> *Asset Allocation:* Determine the right mix of stocks, bonds, and real estate for your stage in life.
>
> *Regular Rebalancing:* Review your portfolio periodically to sell over-performing assets and buy under-performing ones, bringing your allocation back to its intended target.
>
> *Professional Guidance:* Especially for the busy entrepreneur, consulting a financial advisor or investment professional is key to making informed, disciplined decisions.

Building wealth outside your business requires knowledge, patience, and a commitment to the "talk". By diversifying your portfolio and conducting thorough research, you position yourself for long-term success that doesn't depend on you running faster on the treadmill. Regularly review and adjust your strategy as your life and the markets evolve.

12

Investment And Wealth Management

Investing and wealth management play a crucial role in building a solid financial future. However, many individuals shy away from discussing investment strategies due to misconceptions and fears surrounding the topic. For the business owner, this hesitation is often the final barrier to escaping the entrepreneur treadmill. Wealth management is not just about "buying stocks"; it is the strategic process of allocating your resources to generate returns and build wealth that exists independently of your daily labor.

The Significance of Strategic Management
Wealth management involves professionalizing how you handle your capital. For an entrepreneur, this is the process of extracting value from the business to secure the family's future. The significance of this "talk" cannot be overstated:

> *Achieving Financial Goals:* Well-executed strategies accelerate progress toward retirement, home ownership, or funding education.
> *Beating Inflation:* Investing wisely generates returns that outpace inflation, ensuring

your money retains its value over the long term.

Diversifying Income Sources: By allocating funds across stocks, bonds, and real estate, you create multiple streams of income and reduce reliance on your primary business.

Building a Legacy: Effective management ensures your financial impact extends beyond your lifetime to provide for future generations.

Overcoming the Founder's Fears

Before diving into strategies, we must address the common misconceptions and fears that hinder entrepreneurs:

Risk Aversion: Many fear losing hard-earned money. However, a well-diversified portfolio and a long-term perspective mitigate these risks.

Perceived Complexity: Investing is often seen as reserved for experts. With access to professional advice and educational resources, any individual can gain the tools to make informed decisions.

The Timing Myth: Trying to "time the market" is nearly impossible. Success comes from a disciplined, long-term approach rather than chasing short-term fluctuations.

Fear of Losing Control: Wealth management requires striking a balance between investing for growth and maintaining a comfort level that aligns with your personal needs.

Steps for Informed Decision-Making
Building a solid future requires a deep understanding of investment principles.

Define Your Goals: Clarify your short-term and long-term objectives, determining the time horizon and risk tolerance for each.
Diversify and Research: Spread investments across different asset classes and geographic regions to reduce vulnerability. Conduct thorough research on historical performance and future prospects before committing capital.
Seek Professional Advice: If you lack the time or expertise to manage a portfolio, a financial advisor can help develop a tailored plan.
Control Emotions and Taxes: Avoid impulsive decisions based on market noise. Utilize tax-advantaged accounts, such as IRAs or 401(k)s, to minimize liabilities.

The Power of Compounding and Ethical Investing

Compound interest allows your investments to grow exponentially over time. By reinvesting earnings and staying invested for the long term, you harness the full potential of your capital. Furthermore, modern wealth management often includes Ethical and Socially Responsible Investing (ESG). This allows you to align your investments with your personal values—such as environmental stewardship or social justice—while still pursuing financial returns.

Investing is a journey that requires patience, discipline, and ongoing education. By discussing strategies openly, overcoming fears, and making informed decisions, you take control of your financial destiny. Stay focused on your goals, diversify your assets, and leverage the power of compound interest. Incorporating sound practices into your wealth management approach paves the way for a brighter, more secure future.

Transparency Toolkit: The "Wealth Manager" Scripts

Moving from "business owner" to "wealth builder" requires a new set of conversations. Use these scripts to start:

To a Financial Advisor:

"I have been focusing 100% of my energy on running my business, but I realize I haven't professionalized my personal balance sheet. I want to discuss a 'Wealth Extraction' strategy—how

can we move profits from the company into a diversified portfolio that protects my family even if the business hits a rough patch?"

To a Spouse:

"We've been reinvesting everything back into the business for years, but I want to start a conversation about our personal wealth. I'd like us to start a regular contribution to a separate investment account so that we are building a safety net that doesn't depend on my daily presence at the office."

To a Business Partner:

"I think it's important for the health of our partnership that we both have strong personal wealth management strategies in place. If our personal finances are secure, we can make better, less emotional decisions for the business. Can we talk about how we're handling our individual draws and long-term planning?"

13

Cultural Perspectives On Money

Money is not merely a practical tool for transactions; it is a subject deeply intertwined with our culture, shaping our attitudes, beliefs, and behaviors. In Latin America and the Dominican

Republic, the "entrepreneur treadmill" is often a legacy handed down through generations. To truly unlock financial freedom, we must recognize how our cultural background influences our financial perspectives and learn to navigate the taboos that keep us silent.

Cultural Influences on the Treadmill
Our attitudes toward money are significantly impacted by cultural values and socioeconomic backgrounds. In our region, these factors often dictate how we perceive success and how we handle financial conversations:

> *Collective Values (Familismo):* Many cultures prioritize collective well-being, focusing on supporting the extended family and community over individual wealth accumulation. While noble, this can sometimes lead entrepreneurs to stay on the treadmill longer than necessary to meet perceived family obligations.
> *Social Norms and "Politeness":* Many of us grew up in environments where discussing money was considered taboo or impolite. This cultural silence prevents entrepreneurs from seeking the help they need when the treadmill becomes too fast to manage.

Gender Roles: Cultural expectations often shape financial responsibilities within a household. Traditional roles may place the entire burden of financial decision-making on one person, leading to a lack of transparency and increased stress for the "provider" on the treadmill.

Perception of Wealth: Different cultures define success in varying ways, from material possessions to spiritual fulfillment. These definitions impact the goals we strive for and the point at which we feel "successful" enough to step off the treadmill.

Overcoming the Silence in a Family Context
In many families, the business and the household are inseparable. Breaking the silence in this context requires extreme bravery and specific strategies to overcome cultural barriers:

Intergenerational Conversations: We must bridge the gap between older generations, who may hold traditional views on secrecy, and younger generations, who seek transparency. Encouraging parents to share their financial wisdom while allowing children to express their perspectives creates mutual understanding.

The "Legacy" Talk: In families where inheritance is a factor, open conversations about wills and estate planning are essential to prevent future conflict and ensure a smooth transition of wealth. Transparency avoids misunderstandings and resentment down the line.

Creating Safe Spaces: We need to establish environments where family members feel comfortable discussing financial goals and challenges without fear of judgment.

Finding Common Ground Across Cultures
While our perspectives may differ, celebrating this diversity allows for a richer exchange of ideas and financial strategies:

Universal Principles: Regardless of culture, fundamental principles like the importance of saving, budgeting, and managing debt remain constant. These serve as a starting point for any cross-cultural financial dialogue.

Shared Aspirations: Identifying common financial goals across different cultural backgrounds creates a basis for collaborative problem-solving.

Active Listening: Promoting open dialogue and empathetic listening fosters an appreciation for diverse viewpoints.

Collaborative Learning: We can learn from the unique financial practices and traditions of others to enhance our own financial literacy on a global scale.

By understanding cultural influences and overcoming local taboos, we can promote open discussions that lead to greater financial well-being for everyone. Embracing these diverse perspectives allows us to build a more inclusive financial landscape—one where the "entrepreneur treadmill" is recognized as a challenge to be overcome through collective transparency and shared wisdom.

14

Financial Transparency In The Future

The landscape of money talk is evolving rapidly, driven by technological advancements and changing societal norms. In the past, silence was the default; in the future, transparency will be the new gold standard. For the entrepreneur, this shift is critical because the future of business valuation isn't just about what is on your balance sheet—it is about how clearly and honestly that balance sheet is communicated. By understanding and adapting to these changes, we can navigate the financial world more effectively and foster greater well-being for all.

Technology: The Facilitator of the "Talk"
Technology is revolutionizing the way we engage in financial conversations and access financial education. It should never replace the human connection, but it can act as a bridge to make those difficult "Money Matters" conversations easier to start.

> *Digital Financial Platforms:* Online platforms and mobile apps have made financial conversations more accessible and convenient. They allow individuals to manage their finances and engage in discussions within virtual communities.
> *The Power of Real-Time Data:* Personal finance apps make it easier to track spending, set goals, and receive personalized guidance. These tools empower individuals to make informed decisions based on reality rather than guesswork.
> *Interactive Learning:* Gamified platforms and virtual reality (VR) technologies have the potential to transform financial education by simulating real-life scenarios.

This allows individuals to practice high-stakes decision-making in a safe, virtual environment.

Navigating the "Digital Treadmill"
As money talk evolves, new trends and challenges emerge that we must navigate effectively. Without open dialogue, these complex new systems can quickly become another trap on the treadmill.

> *Cryptocurrencies and Blockchain* : These technologies are disrupting traditional systems and challenging conventional notions of money. Understanding these implications is essential for any informed discussion about the future of finance.
> *The Changing Work Landscape:* The rise of the gig economy and remote work brings unique challenges like income volatility. Future money talk must address retirement planning and benefits for these non-traditional arrangements.
> *Privacy and Data Security:* As transactions move online, ensuring the security of personal and financial information becomes a paramount concern in every conversation.

The Transparency Mandate

To create a more inclusive world, we must champion transparency as a core principle. This isn't just about individual wealth; it is about building a trustworthy financial ecosystem for the generations to come.

Financial Inclusion: We must advocate for bridging the gap between underserved communities and mainstream financial services.

Sustainable and Impact Investing: There is a growing shift toward aligning financial decisions with environmental, social, and governance (ESG) factors. Engaging in discussions about the *impact* of our investments is becoming increasingly important.

Transparent Financial Services: We must encourage institutions to prioritize transparency in their products, ensuring that terms, fees, and risks are always clearly understood.

A Call to Action for Positive Change

The future of money talk is marked by technological progress, but its success depends on our willingness to remain human. By working together and embracing transparency, we turn money talk into a powerful tool for empowerment and positive change.

Engaging in Public Discourse: We must actively participate in conversations about financial policies and societal norms.
Leading by Example: By being a vocal advocate for transparency, we can collectively shape a more informed and inclusive financial landscape.

Money Matters Note: As we embrace the opportunities that technology offers, we must remain mindful of the human values that guide us. Transparency is not just a trend—it is the foundation of true financial freedom and a brighter future for all.